'90 GROUP GUIDE

GROUP D

Milan Bologna

W.GERMANY UAE YUGOSLAVIA COLOMBIA

DATE	VENUE	TIME	TEAMS	RESULT
June 9	Bologna	8pm	UAE v Colombia	
June 10	Milan	8pm	West Germany v Yugoslavia	
June 14	Bologna	4pm	Yugoslavia v Colombia	
June 15	Milan	8pm	West Germany v UAE	
June 19	Milan	4pm	West Germany v Colombia	
June 19	Bologna	4pm	Yugoslavia v UAE	

GROUP E

Verona Udine

BELGUIM URUGUAY SPAIN S.KOREA

DATE	VENUE	TIME	TEAMS	RESULT
June 12	Verona	4pm	Belgium v South Korea	
June 13	Udine	4pm	Uruguay v Spain	
June 17	Verona	8pm	Belgium v Uruguay	
June 17	Udine	8pm	South Korea v Spain	
June 21	Verona	4pm	Belgium v Spain	
June 21	Udine	4pm	South Korea v Uruguay	

GROUP F

Cagliari Palermo

ENGLAND HOLLAND REP. OF IRELAND EGYPT

DATE	VENUE	TIME	TEAMS	RESULT
June 11	Cagliari	8pm	England v Rep of Ireland	
June 12	Palermo	8pm	Holland v Egypt	
June 16	Cagliari	8pm	England v Holland	
June 17	Palermo	4pm	Rep of Ireland v Egypt	
June 21	Cagliari	8pm	England v Egypt	
June 21	Palermo	8pm	Rep of Ireland v Holland	

...en against Austria the following day. June 11 sees ...osta Rica. Kick-offs given in British Summer Time.

ISBN 1-85613-016-9

Manufactured in Spain

Producer: Ted Smart
Author: Albert Sewell
Book Design: Sara Cooper
Production Assistant: Seni Glaister

My special thanks to **Steve Powell**, MD of Allsport;
and to **Tony Graham**, Allsport, who researched
all of the photographs.

All photographs © Allsport.
3 Greenlea Park, Prince George's Rd.,
London SW19 2JP England.
081-685-1010

Photographers whose photographs appear in this book:

David Cannon - Simon Bruty - Ben Radford -
Richiardi - Gray Mortimore - Bob Martin -
Cor Mody - Inpho - Russell Cheyne -
Michael King - Billy Stickland -
Mike Powell.

THE WORLD CUP 1990

Text by
ALBERT SEWELL

TED SMART

WORLD CUP PREVIEW

ALBERT SEWELL

I am really looking forward to the start of the World Cup Finals so that we can all enjoy again the thrills and excitement which make this great competition unique.

The contrast between the various nations is always fascinating. The skill and finesse of the South Americans, the technique and efficiency of the Europeans and the workrate and strength of the Britons provide an enthralling mixture. And don't forget the sheer enjoyment which is brought to the tournament by the lesser-known countries from African, Asian and Concacaf countries.

All of these ingredients make up an exciting cocktail and predicting the winners is virtually impossible. Of the 24 qualifiers, at least 16 — including England and Scotland — have reasons to believe they might claim the famous trophy on July 8.

Providing Brazil, West Germany, Holland and Italy avoid each other in the earlier rounds, they are the four teams I would expect to reach the semi-finals. Assuming West Germany and Holland do not meet in the semi-finals, then they are the teams I expect to contest the final, with my money on Holland.

The European Champions, more than any other team, have a nucleus of players who would be automatic choices for any one of the 24 competing countries. Which international manager would even consider leaving out Ruud Gullit, Marco Van Basten, Frank Rijkaard or Ronald Koeman? As long as they are all fit, Holland may prove unbeatable... as well as providing some superb television entertainment.

Franz Beckenbauer's West Germany will be as formidable as ever.They seem always to produce the goods when it matters and are highly respected for their skill, tactical awareness and never-say-die attitude. Their captain Lothar Matthaus is one to watch and he is part of a strong midfield trio which also includes Brehme and Moller.

Brazil have reportedly got their strongest squad for years. In Muller, Romario, Careca and Bebeto they have four of the best strikers in the world, and goalkeeper Taffarel is arguably the finest stopper the country has produced since Gilmar in the 1950's and 60's.

The hosts Italy are the bookmakers' favourites, though they will need to be able to cope with the pressure of playing in front of their own fanatical supporters. As always, their side is built on solid defence where sweeper Franco Baresi will be a key man, but they also have some fine, young attackers — Gianluca Vialli has developed into an excellent striker and Roberto Baggio's unpredictable skills have led to him being compared to England's Paul Gascoigne.

We should be optimistic about England's chances. Bobby Robson has done well in guiding us to the Finals again but now we need evidence that the European Championship debacle of two years ago is well behind us. Players like captain Bryan Robson, keeper Peter Shilton and central defender Terry Butcher will be the cornerstone of our hopes, but Gascoigne, if given his chance could be the jewel in our crown.

Scotland keep qualifying — this is the fifth time in succession they have reached the finals but then they continually disappoint us. Indeed, they have never reached the second phase. There is no doubt that they have the players to do well. Rangers' team-mates Maurice Johnston and Ally McCoist are a potent attacking partnership and Steve Nicol and Paul McStay are both excellent players.

The Republic of Ireland are in the Finals for the first time and there is no doubt that they will enjoy themselves. They surprised everybody in the 1988 European Championship in West Germany and it will be interesting to see if they can reproduce that form and enjoy similar success.

Champions Argentina will need Diego Maradona at his best if they are to emulate Brazil's 1958 achievement of winning the World Cup in Europe, but nonetheless, they will be a difficult side to beat. Every country will have something to offer. Yugoslavia and Spain could both spring a surprise. Yugoslavia's Dragan Stojkovic is a superb midfield playmaker and could emerge as one of the stars of the tournament while Spain have a proven goalscorer, a valuable asset, in Emilio Butragueno.

Czechoslovakia are another dark horse. Despite losing 4 - 2 to England at Wembley in April, they were sufficiently impressive to suggest that they could be a threat.

Sweden do not travel well but in Glenn Hysen they have a defender of a true world class. Belgium, semi-finalists in 1986, still have the dangerous Jan Ceulemans leading their attack, but are unlikely to repeat their achievement of four years ago.

Uruguay could do well providing they control their volatile tempers and their fellow South Americans, Colombia, will certainly provide one of the characters of the tournament in Carlos Valderrama, their dreadlocked striker.

Romania and Russia will be typically efficient and hard to break down and Austria, with Toni Polster up front, could shock a few people.

At the other end of the scale, Costa Rica, USA, South Korea, Cameroon, Egypt and the United Arab Emirates may not win too many matches but if past experience is anything to go by, they will win many fans.

All in all, it promises to be a feast of football. Let battle commence and may the best team win.

Albert Sewell has been football statistician/researcher for BBC Television (Grandstand, Match of the Day, Sportsnight) since 1968 and is now coming up to his sixth World Cup with the BBC.

Opposite : Maradona and Trophy

16

THE GLORY OF THE PAST
Wembley 1966

Opposite Top: 1966 World Cup Final. England celebrate victory with Bobby Moore. **Opposite Bottom:** Martin Peters scores Englands 2nd goal with Geoff Hurst celebrating. **Above Left & Right:** Bobby Moore and Jack Charlton celebrate victory. **Below:** Geoff Hursts controversial 3rd goal for England. **Bottom Right :** Bobby Moore with the World Cup Trophy with Gorden Banks celebrating.

The 1970 Legend of Pele

Opposite Top and Bottom : 1970 World Cup Final, Mexico. Pele in action for Brazil. **Above Right :** Pele shoots for goal. **Above Left :** Pele is surrounded by Italians after foul. **Right :** Pele shoots for goal.

1974 Beckenbauer & Cruyff

Right and below: Cruyff fouled (penalty)

Beckenbauer with the World Cup Trophy

Neeskens scores

World Cup 1986. Aztec Stadium

Italian far

WORLD CUP
1982 in Spain

Marco Tardelli celebrates.

Paulo Rossi (Italy) scores

Zoff and Gentile

Paulo Rossi. World Cup Finals 1982.

Manager
Carlos Bilardo

ARGENTINA

Group B
Milan Naples Bari

The success of Carlos Bilardo and his men in Mexico four years ago booked Argentina's place in Italy. That was their second World Cup triumph in three tournaments. In 1978 they overcame Holland 3 - 1, after extra time, in front of their own fiercely patriotic fans at the River Plate Stadium in Buenos Aires. Then, in Mexico in 1986, they beat West Germany 3 - 2 in a truly outstanding match.

Since that victory, the team has been largely rebuilt. They still have Diego Maradona, but even though he will now, barring injury, be playing in Italy, he cannot expect to pull the 'hand of God' stroke again. The two footballing sides of Maradona were on very public show in the 1986 World Cup quarter-final against England. The first goal was scored with his hand; his inspired second was a magnificent solo effort.

John Burruchaga, who scored Argentina's third in the 1986 final, has been plagued with injuries with Nantes, but centre-forward Diaz could be important to them if his reported feud with Maradona is sorted out in good time for these Finals. Watch, too, for the up and coming right-winger Claudio Cannigia.

As they have not been required to play in a competitive qualifying group, it is difficult to gauge quite how potent a force Argentina will be in Italy, Last year they were a great disappointment in the South American Cup, finishing third behind Brazil and Uruguay and scoring just two goals in seven matches. Maradona summed up his team's sentiments after that tournament, saying: "It was certainly not a very happy time for us, I didn't enjoy it much at all." Suggesting, perhaps, that Argentina are vulnerable this time round.

Argentina Team Group

Valdano/Hodge (England)

Fenwick/Maradona

Giusti/Magath (West Germany)

Nery Pompido

Diego Maradonna

Maradonna - Matthaus

Claudio Canaggia

Voller scores

Valdano score

Maradona

Maradona

Maradona

VERDICT:

Their defence of the World Cup will hinge on Mardona being one hundred per cent.

Manager
Joseph (Pepi) Hickersberger

AUSTRIA

Group A
Rome Florence

Qualification was a vindication of the much-criticised methods employed by manager Joseph Hickersberger. Just over a year ago he was under fire as his side trailed in the table behind the USSR, the eventual Group 3 winners, and the resurgent Turkey. In desperation, the manager persuaded Herbert Prohaska, the 34-year-old former Austrian 'golden boy', to come out of retirement.

The last-gasp effort worked, Austria remained in contention and a hat-trick in the final match from the new star of Austrian international football, Seville forward Toni Polster, secured qualification as group runners-up. A speedy forward capable of unlocking any defence, Polster will put his experience of Spanish football to good use in Italy.

However, Austria's disappointing record of only one goal scored in four away qualifiers may douse the threat posed by Polster. The Austrians must maintain the supply to him if he is to shine, and they are to progress, in Italy.

Austria last appeared in the World Cup finals in Spain eight years ago, when group rivals Algeria made an official protest to FIFA, questioning the 'lack of effort' shown by Austrian and West German players in a decisive match in Gijon. The Germans' 1 - 0 victory meant both Europeans qualified for the second stage of the tournament while Algeria were eliminated on goal difference.

Austria Team Group

Polster

Andreas Ogris

Klaus Lindenberger

VERDICT:

Will have the problem of providing an adequate supply for star striker Polster.

Manager
Walter Meeuws

BELGUIM

Group E
Verona Udine

Although unfancied, Belgium have made a habit of upsetting the odds in major tournaments. Many of the qualifiers waited anxiously to hear whether Belgium, beaten finalists in the 1980 European Championship and semi-finalists in the 1986 World Cup, were to be seeded in Italy.

An unbeaten record in Group 7 was blemished only by their failure to beat no-hopers Luxembourg in their final. The disappointment of that 1 - 1 draw will give new manager Guy Thys, plenty to think about.

Nico Claesen, now back in Belgium following his stint with Tottenham Hotspur, will lead a Belgian attack, which still draws upon the huge experience of veteran World Cup campaigner Jan Ceulemans. Ceulemans, remember, scored against England in a 1 - 1 draw in the 1980 European Championship in Italy.

Belgium's total of 15 goals was better than most of the European qualifiers, but they would be much more content if they had not drawn as many as four matches. In the 1986 World Cup finals, en route to a semi-final defeat by eventual winners Argentina, Belgium figured in the tournament's most exciting match. A 4 - 3 second round win against the USSR took Belgium into the quarter-finals.

That will possibly be as far as they progress in Italy.

Belgium World Cup Squad

Jan Ceulemans

Nico Clausen

Michel Preud'Homme

VERDICT:

Will not get as far as last time.

Manager
Sebastiao Lazaroni

BRAZIL

Group C
Turin Genoa

Brazil Team Group

Brazilian Fans

The only country to have participated in every World Cup, Brazil go to Italy as unbeaten winners of South American Group 3. International football demands a successful Brazilian side. They exude skill and excitement in equal measure and will revel on the world stage this summer.

Crowned kings of world football three times, Brazil have not reached the final since 1970, when Italy were magically swept aside 4 - 1 by Pele and company. Their 1 - 0 victory against Uruguay in the 1989 South American championship, their first major success since that 1970 World Cup, lifted Brazilian morale. Rio's teeming millions are praying that Brazil can repeat the achievement of

1958, when, in Sweden, they became the first, and so far only, South American side to have won the World Cup on European soil.

With more than half their current players now with European clubs, the team should be well prepared for the conditions. The European contingent includes the likes of Dunga, Careca, Valdo, Silas and Romario, who scored the South American championship winner against Uruguay. Bebeto, a new shooting star in the South American qualifying rounds, is emerging as a forward of brilliance and will be one to look out for in Italy.

Manager Sebastiao Lazaroni's appointment for the finals was confirmed only when Brazil clinched the South American championship — up until then he had been under great pressure from both fans and media. Whether he continues beyond 1990 will depend on their World Cup performance this summer.

Joao Paulo (Brazil), Mikhial Itchenko (Russia)

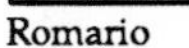
Romario

Branco

Paulo Roberto

Careca

Milton Silva

G. Silva

Romario (Brazil) Victor Lossev (USSR)

Giresse/Elzo

Careca (II)

Alamao

VERDICT:

Expect South America's strongest challenge to come from them... and they are overdue another World Cup success.

Manager
Valeri Nepomniaschi

CAMEROON

Group B
Milan Naples Bari

Cameroon clinched the second African qualifying place with their 3 - 0 victory over two legs against Tunisia last year and go to Italy with a proud World Cup record. Their only previous appearance in the Finals, in Spain in 1982, resulted in three drawn matches — an accomplished performance in a group which included eventual winners Italy and third-placed Poland.

The African Champions mix strong defence with fast, flamboyant attack under the tactical leadership of Russian coach Valeri Mepomniaschi. The 41-year-old Siberian took charge of Cameroon in January 1989 after coaching a Soviet second division team.

Mepomniaschi guided them to the finals by overcoming Angola, Gabon and Nigeria in group competition before the decisive play-off victories against Tunisia, 2 - 0 in Yaounde and 1 - 0 in Tunis. The victory guaranteed big rewards from the national government and several players will now use these finals as their passport into the lucrative world of European football.

Cameroon's key player could be experienced goalkeeper Antoine Bell who was understudy to 'The Spider' Thomas N'Kono in 1982 and has regularly come close to winning the African player of the year award.

Cameroon Team Group

Edwele Bertin

Makanaky

Cyrille Makanky

VERDICT:

Will be homeward bound after stage one - gone but not forgotten.

Manager
Francisco Maturana

COLOMBIA

Group D
Milan Bologna

Colombia, in the finals for the first time since 1962, promise to be one of the most colourful teams in Italy. With Rene Higuita, a goalkeeper who doubles as penalty-taker, and Carlos Valderrama, — the 'South American Gullit' — their matches are sure to be packed with drama and excitement. Venezuela will vouch for Higuita's deadly accuracy from the penalty spot — he scored against them in last summer's Copa America, the South American championship.

Unusually, Valderrama, the Colombian captain and midfield creator-in-chief, did not shine in the Copa America. Colombia disappointed and failed to reach the semi-finals but two years earlier, during the 1987 championship, the brilliance of the French-based forward had helped him become the first Colombian winner of the South American Footballer of the Year award. On that side of the world they say Valderrama has the most stunning dribbling skill since Pele!

Qualification was guaranteed when winger Albeiro Uzurriago scored the only goal of a two-legged South America/Oceania play-off with Israel. In the qualifying rounds, Arnoldo Iguaran was their top-scorer, with four goals. Manager Francisco Maturana, appointed in 1986, represented Colombia in the 1978 and 1982 World Cup qualifying competitions. Most of his side in Italy will come from one club, Nacional, and the experience of playing together regularly will stand them in good stead this summer.

World Cup Squad

Higuita (Chile)

Valderramma

Albeiro Uzuriaga

VERDICT:

Their preparation has been upset by domestic upheavals since they qualified.

COSTA RICA

Manager
Marvin Rodriguez

Group C
Turin Genoa

Making their first appearance in the World Cup, new boys Costa Rica will do well to win a game. Rest assured, though, they will play their hearts out. Eight demanding games in the Concacaf qualifying section saw them travel great distances — for instance, to North America to take on the United States and to the Caribbean, where they met Trinidad & Tobago — and new manager Bora Milutinovic will be hoping that all their travels were worth while.

Unbeaten at home in San Jose, they enjoyed a break in the second round of the qualification tournament with a walk-over against Mexico, who had been banned from the competition after playing over-age players in an international youth tournament.

But the Costa Ricans had some uncomfortable moments away from home, particularly when they were pelted with objects by the crowd as they beat El Salvador 4 - 2 last June. Three weeks later a header by Pastor Fernandez gave them the win in the return match which virtually guaranteed qualification and the celebrations began.

On October 8, they brought out the champagne at their training camp in Italy, where they had gone for some early conditioning, when the USA drew 0 - 0 with Guatemala — a result that confirmed Costa Rica's qualification.

World Cup Squad

VERDICT:

A major achievement by them would be to reach the second phase.

EGYPT

Manager
El-Gohary

Group F
Cagliari Palermo

Egyptian Team Group

Egypt are making a return visit to Italy, 56 years after qualifying for their first, and only, World Cup finals, in 1934, when they became Africa's initial representatives on the world stage. Then they were limited to one game, a 4 - 2 defeat by Hungary. This time they are guaranteed at least three matches, to the delight of their fanatical supporters.

A crowd of 125,000 at Cairo's National Stadium on November 17 1989 saw them beat Algeria 1 - 0 to qualify for the finals. The referee, Ali Benaceur, could not leave the pitch until eight minutes after his final whistle, such was the pandemonium as the crowd lit newspapers, threw fruit and danced in celebration.

The euphoria was not surprising. Algeria had qualified for the previous two World Cups and were favourites to do so again. Egypt had won their qualifying group to reach the play-offs, and then held Algeria to 0 - 0 in the away leg. Their vital goal in the return game was scored by centre-forward Hossaim Hassan in the fourth minute. Excellent displays from full-backs Ibrahim Hassan and Raby Yasim ensured that Egypt hung on to their slender lead until the final whistle.

Egypt's two top clubs, El-Ahly and Zamalek, provide the bulk of the squad of players who will travel to Italy. On the field, discipline could be a problem.

Former Wales manager Mike Smith will be particularly interested in their progress — he was their coach for three years and led them to victory in the 1986 African Nations Cup.

VERDICT:

The company they are in makes them bankers to finish bottom of group F.

Manager
Josef Venglos

CZECHOSLOVAKIA

Group A
Rome Florence

Having missed out on Mexico in 1986, the Czechs qualified for the 1990 World Cup finals by finishing second in European Group 7, level on points with Belgium, and with one more victory than the group winners. For their manager, Dr Josef Venglos, it was a huge relief.

With Switzerland and Luxembourg as the 'easy' teams in their group, it was always likely that any two of Czechoslovakia, Belgium and Portugal would qualify. As it turned out, by the time Portugal were held to a goalless draw in November, Venglos's team had assured themselves of a place in Italy.

Among the names to look out for in the Czechoslovak side is Sparta Prague's Griga. Although the striker had a lean patch in the qualifying tournament, he is a proven goalscorer who hit the target 16 times in 27 Under-21 appearances. He has been described as the Gerd Muller of Czechoslovakia.

Their World Cup preparations were not eased by the problems which surrounded the defection of two key players — Lubos Kubik and Ivo Knoflicek — and their subsequent abortive attempt to sign for Derby County. However, in the more open political climate which has since developed, things became more stable and the team will be able to have a more concentrated approach to this World Cup than seemed possible at one time.

Last time the tournament was held in Italy, in 1934, Czechoslovakia reached the Final, losing 2 - 1 to the host country in extra time. They were also beaten Finalists in 1962 — by Brazil in Chile.

Czechoslovakia Team Group

Jan Stejskal

Stanislav Griga

Josef Chovanek

VERDICT:

Just a hunch - 'possibles' for a semi-finals place.

Manager
Bobby Robson

ENGLAND

Group F
Cagliari Palermo

England Team Group

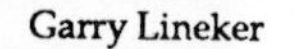

Garry Lineker

John Barnes

The memory of the 1988 European Championship lies heavy on English shoulders. That humiliation in those Finals of two years ago in West Germany, where a 100 per cent record of defeat ridiculed Bobby Robson's expectations, subsequently united the squad. They abhorred the criticism that was flung at them and vowed to restore faith in English football. They now have the chance of repeating their World Cup triumph of 1966.

England claimed one of two qualifying places reserved for 'best runners-up' in groups of four countries and are the only team not have conceded a goal during qualification. Outstanding performances in Sweden and Poland from Peter Shilton, proved that, despite breaking the 40-year age barrier, he is still England's number one.

Bobby Robson had eight months from the date of qualification to decide what was needed to turn England from qualifiers into possible World Cup winners. Controversy raged over Paul Gascoigne. If Gascoigne has 'grown up' sufficiently in Robson's eyes, he must play, for, as he showed with his display against Czechoslovakia in April of this year, here is a footballer who can make all the difference to the length of England's stay in Italy. The return to fitness of the Manchester United midfield men Bryan Robson and Neil Webb is an added boost for the manager.

Robson should also be prepared to give John Barnes the freedom which he enjoys with Liverpool. If allowed to roam in a central attacking position, Barnes can open up the best defences in the world, but on the wing he is drowned in a sea of legs and markers.

Robson will be hoping for a repeat of Gary Lineker's Mexico performance of four years ago, when he was the World Cup top scorer with six goals. The combination of Barnes, in a different role, and Lineker could solve the scoring problems that have afflicted England of late. The only away goals scored in the qualifying round were the two that beat Albania. Becoming World Champions demands much, much more.

Garry Lineker scores

Peter Shilton

Bryan Robson

McLeish (Scotland) Walker (England)

Garry Lineker

Chris Waddle

John Barnes (England) Prusik (Poland)

umbro

Peter Shilton Peter Beardsley Garry Lineker

Simpson (Scotland) Robson (England) Butcher (England) Pereira (Portugal)

Garry Lineker scores

Garry Lineker

Neil Webb

Mark Wright

Steve McMahon

Peter Shilton

Peter Beardsley

VERDICT:

Unaccustomed problems for Bobby Robson - too many players demanding selection. Could reach the last four.... then who knows?

Manager
Thijs Libregts

HOLLAND

Group F
Cagliari Palermo

Currently European Champions, the Dutch are one of the favourites to win in Italy. Manager Leo Beenhakker, who recently replaced Thijs Libregts — who in turn took over from Rinus Michels after the 1988 European conquest, has a marvellous assembly of individual skills at his disposal.

A fully fit Ruud Gullit — 1987 European Footballer of the Year, Marco Van Basten — Gullit's successor to that title in 1988, Ronald Koeman and Frank Rijkaard would grace the greatest teams. Van Basten's star shone brightest in West Germany two years ago as the Milan forward returned from injury to become the top-scorer. His five goals included three in the humiliation of England and an unforgetable volley in the final against the USSR.

The big worry in season 1989-90 was Van Basten's Milan team-mate and captain, the dreadlocked Gullit. He inspired Milan to victory in the 1989 European Cup Final, but in doing so aggravated his knee injury and did not play in the first half of the new season. Holland qualified for the finals as unbeaten winners of Group 4, beating West Germany into second place. Two appearances in World Cup finals have seen two defeats, losing to hosts West Germany and Argentina in 1974 and 1978 respectively. The 1990 finals could well be third time lucky.

Holland Team Group

Van Basten

Ruud Gullit

KNVB

Ruud Gullit

Rijkaard

Aerle

Ruud Gullit

Vannenburg

Van Basten

Holland fans

Koeman

VERDICT:

The European Champions have never won the world cup... will probably do it given a fit Gullit.

Manager
Azeglio Vicini

ITALY

Group A
Rome Florence

As hosts, Italy will receive fanatical support but will be under extra pressure to succeed — the penalty for failure will be high. Five host nations have won the World Cup, including Italy themselves in 1934 — the last time they staged the finals. Two more Italian victories followed in 1938 and 1982. Now they kick-off the 1990 tournament as favourites.

Free from the pressure of qualifying, coach Azeglio Vicini has used a series of friendly internationals and Under-21 matches to rebuild the side which was eliminated in the second stage of the 1986 finals.

To many, the most exciting prospect in the new Italian team is Roberto Baggio. He burst on to the scene when he beat man after man, to score a brilliant goal for Fiorentina in Naples. Five days later Baggio, playing just behind the front two, scored twice and made another, as Italy beat Bulgaria 4 - 0 in Cesena. However, such is Italy's strength in depth he is not guaranteed a place in the team. Vicini is known to be considering using him as an out-and-out forward alongside Italy's main goalscoring hope, Gianluca Vialli, of Sampdoria. Since gaining his place in the Italian squad for Mexico in 1986, Vialli has matured into a world-class striker. His 40th cap for Italy came in November 1989, and he may well have two good reasons to celebrate his 26th birthday this year — the day after the World Cup Final!

With Walter Zenga, the vastly experienced Inter Milan goalkeeper, guarding the net and sweeper Franco Baresi, a strong, authoritative player, marshalling his troops, Italy's defence will, as usual, be one of their strongest points.

The 1990 World Cup is Italy's own party. They will not relinquish the limelight without a fight.

Italy Team Group

Giuseppe Giannini

Luca Fusi

De Napoli

Baggio

Guiseppe Giannini

Luigi De Agostini

Walther Zeng

Roberto Donadoni

Gianluca Vialli

F Baresi

Malinho/Carnevale

Gianluca Vialli

Serena

VERDICT:

Could become the first host country to become World Champions twice.

Manager
Jack Charlton

REPUBLIC OF IRELAND

Group F
Cagliari Palermo

February 1986 was a good month for Irish football. Jack Charlton succeeded Eoin Hand as Republic of Ireland manager and the team have enjoyed non-stop glory ever since. Apart from success on the field, the Football Association of Ireland's bank account has been swelled to overflowing. So much so that there is talk of building a 50,000 all-seater stadium in Dublin for the team that has no home of its own. The fairytale began with qualification for the 1988 European Championship, the first time they had reached the final of a major tournament. They arrived in West Germany with few people expecting them to pose much of a threat but their direct brand of football turned the predictions on their heads. They missed out on a semi-final place by a matter of minutes only when Holland's Wim Kieft deflected Ronald Koeman's shot into the bottom corner of the net.

It was cruel luck on the Republic but they returned from Germany as national heroes and Charlton was declared 'an honorary Irishman' by Premier Charles Haughey. Now big Jack has led his adopted country to their first World Cup finals and large numbers of devoted fans are expected to make the trip to Italy.

Charlton developed the direct style which the team ably transformed into results. With players of the class of Ronnie Whelan, Frank Stapleton and Kevin Sheedy in their ranks, coupled with Charlton's own experience as a World Cup winner with England in 1966, the Republic have the ability to test any opposition.

Stapleton, who joined QPR's Don Givens as the country's top scorer with 19 goals, can bring vast experience to the heat of World Cup battle, while Whelan and Sheedy, along with Ray Houghton, pull the strings in midfield. The Republic booked their place in the finals with a 2 - 0 win over Malta in Valetta, with John Aldridge scoring both goals.

Republic of Ireland Team Group

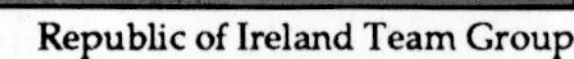

Jack Charlton (Manager)

Tony Cascrarino

John Aldridge

World Cup Qualifier Malta (0) Eire (2)

Ray Houghton

Paul McGrath

Ronnie Whelan

Kevin Sheedy

Houghton and Moran

John Aldridge

Ronnie Whelan

Frank Stapleton

David O'Leary

Eire celebrate own goal by Michel/Spain

VERDICT:

Nobody knows how far they might go - we all know no-one will enjoy playing against them.

Manager
Emerich Jenei

ROMANIA

Group B
Milan Naples Bari

An act of petulance in the decisive 3 - 1 Group 1 defeat of Denmark in the qualifiers led to Gheorghe Hagi, the Romanian captain and midfield inspiration, being sent off. The resulting one-match suspension will operate in the opening match in Italy, and his ban dampened celebrations that accompanied Romania's qualification for the finals for the first time since 1970.

Hagi's influence cannot be understated. At 19, he was a key member of the 1984 European Championship team in France. Few doubt that he will follow Ladislau Boloni and become the second Romanian to win 100 caps. England have cause to remember Hagi from the torment he gave Bobby Robson's defence in two qualifiers for the 1986 World Cup finals.

In the initial absence of Hagi, manager Emerich Jenei will expect six foot three inch forward Marcel Coras, a revelation in the 1984 European Championship, to take centre stage in attack.

Romania's players may well be inspired by the new freedoms at home long-term prospects in Italy may hinge on the quality of their defence. In two qualifying ties against Denmark, the only top-flight opposition in that group, they conceded four goals. They can expect to be heavily punished for similar lapses in Italy.

Romania Team Group

Sabau

Marius Lacatus

Hagi

Marius Lacatus

Gheorghe Popescu

Klein (Romania), Balkov (Bulgaria)

VERDICT:

Hard to beat, and even harder to see them going far.

Manager
Andy Roxburgh

SCOTLAND

Group C
Turin Genoa

Qualification for a fifth successive time for the Scots — quite an achievement for such a small country (in terms of population and geography). Whatever happens you can be sure of one thing, Scotland, whose fervent fans are renowned the world over, will not be under-supported in Italy. Tartan flags and accents to match are sure to be strongly in evidence.

Unfortunately these fervent supporters have yet to be rewarded by the efforts of their team — 1974 saw them miss out on goal difference from Brazil and Yugoslavia, in 1978, they lost to a badly underestimated Peru and drew with Iran only by virtue of an own-goal, 1982 saw them finish third in a tough group which included Brazil and USSR and four years ago, in Mexico, progress was abruptly halted by a cynical Uruguayan team.

This time, they have been guided through by Andy Roxburgh, whose appointment to the job of national team coach — he refuses to be titled 'manager' — in July 1986 left most Scots asking: "Andy who?" He succeeded Alex Ferguson, who was acting-manager for the 1986 finals following the death of Jock Stein.

As usual, Scotland have qualified the hard way. Just as they strung out their 1986 qualification to a play-off with Australia, they gave their fans plenty of nail-biting moments in their group before a 1 - 1 draw with Norway at Hampden Park in their last fixture secured their trip to the finals.

Maurice Johnston, the Rangers and former Celtic striker, now holds the all-time Scottish World Cup scoring record. His total of eight goals in two campaigns takes him past Kenny Dalglish and Joe Jordan. Another striker of whom opponents will have to be wary is Ally McCoist, who scored in the 1 - 1 draw with Norway which cemented qualification. best third places.

Scotland World Cup Squad

Andy Roxburgh (Manager)and Craig Brown(Asst)

Ally McCoist

Jim Leighton

Stuart McKimmie

Richard Gough

Ally McCoist

Alan McInally

Alex McLeish

Willie Miller

Steve Nicol

Mo Johnston

Paul McStay

Durie scores

VERDICT:

Their problem isn't getting to the finals but staying. With Brazil and Sweden in their group they must hipw for one of the best third places.

Manager
Lee Hoe-Taik

SOUTH KOREA

Group E
Verona Udine

South Korea, a football country with no professionals and players who mostly turn out in factory teams, proudly take their place in the World Cup finals for the second time running. In Mexico in 1986, they recovered from a 3 - 1 defeat against Argentina to draw 1 - 1 with Bulgaria and then push Italy hard in a 2 - 3 defeat. South Korea did not progress to the second round, but won plenty of friends with their fast, skilful football.

In East Asia Group 4 they overpowered their rivals in the qualifying stage, scoring 25 goals without reply. Home advantage saw them inflict a 9 - 0 drubbing on Nepal and 3 - 0 defeats of Singapore and Malaysia. Choi Soon Ho, who has aroused the interest of a number of European clubs, was well in evidence on the Koreans' goal trail, while goalkeepers Byung Deuk and Poong Joo, who played in alternate games, were virtual spectators.

The action moved to Singapore for the Asian group play-offs in which the top two countries qualified for Italy. South Korea topped the six-team group, victorious in three games, (including a 1 - 0 win over North Korea) and drawing the other two. They conceded only one goal in 11 games during the qualification process and will add an exciting extra dimension to the finals.

Gu Sang Bum

Kim Joo Sung

South Korea Team Group

Hwang Seon-Hung (S. Korea), Abuulla Aldosari (SAU)

VERDICT:

It will be a surprise of the tournament if they survive the qualifying group.

Manager
Valery Lobanovsky

SOVIET UNION

Group B
Milan Naples Bari

Despite appearing in past finals six times since 1958, the Soviet Union have yet to finish in the first three. But as they showed in the 1988 European Championship, in which they lost 2 - 0 in the Final to Holland, they have truly 'arrived' at international level.

More than half of that 1988 team remains, and the Soviet Union will be no-one's pushovers in Italy. Manager Valery Lobanovsky, who took over before the 1986 World Cup, can depend on his team attacking in style, with Oleg Protasov a proven goalscorer.

The Soviets also appear to have finlly lost their habit of falling apart in defence, as they did against Belgium in Mexico last time, when, despite Belanov's hat-trick, they lost 4 - 3 in extra time. Their defence was breached just four times in eight qualifying games for this World Cup, but a place in the finals was not confirmed until Protasov's two goals beat Turkey in Simferopol in their last match.

For the first time, the Soviets will be able to call upon players who have gained experience in club football abroad. The relaxation in the system means that the likes of Sergei Aleinikov and Alexander Zavarov, with Juventus, and Rinat Dassayev, with Seville, could add vital know-how to the Soviet cause. More than ever before, the USSR could be genuine dark horses for the World Cup.

Russian Team Group

Turkey v Russia

R. Dassayev

Protaso

4
PIYANG

Gennady Litovchenko

Protasov

Tchrerednik

Alexander Zavarov

Mikhal Itchenko

Lujnii

Zavarov

Vasily Rats

VERDICT:

Have to be thought of as possible semi-finalists.

Manager
Luis Suarez

SPAIN

Group E
Verona Udine

Considering the strength of their domestic game it is surprising that Spain have never even reached the semi-finals of the World Cup. But, apart from the hosts, they will be most suited to the conditions in Italy and could be a fair bet to make overdue impact.

In Emilio Butragueno, nicknamed 'The Vulture' because of his goalscoring prowess, they have one of the most lethal strikers in the business. Last time, in Mexico, the Real Madrid star scored five in the finals, one fewer than Gary Lineker, including a remarkable four-goal haul against Denmark. It ended with Spain beaten by Belgium, 5 - 4 on penalties, in the quarter-finals. Only a handful of that team, including goalkeeper Andoni Zubizarreta and forward Julio Salinas, are still in contention for places. At 28, Zubizarreta was the oldest player in the side that completed the qualifying round with a 4 - 0 win against Hungary.

Some exciting replacements have now graduated to the team. Miguel Michel, of Real Madrid, has the skill, finesse and vision to turn a match. He can be one of the most influential midfield players in these finals. Jose Maria Bakero has the assured first touch which can set up an attack in a split-second and Rafael Martin Vasquez is another accomplished midfield player.

Only three goals were scored against Spain on the road to Italy, and as group winners the Spaniards were Europe's top scorers in the qualifying stage with 20 goals in eight matches.

Manager Luis Suarez, appointed after the 1988 European Championships, has a talented team. If they can stay cooler than most in the Italian heat, it could add up to Spain's boldest World Cup showing yet.

Spain Team Group

Butragueno

Enrique Quique

Martin Vaquez

Tomas Sanchiz

Michel

Emilio Butragueno

Quique

Andoni Zubizarreta

Alberto Gorriz

Beguiristain

Manuel Jimenez

Michel

Emilio Butragueno

Gordillo

VERDICT:

A real World Cup show by them is long overdue.

Manager
Olle Nordin

SWEDEN

Group C
Turin Genoa

Like England, whom they denied top place in the final Group 2 qualifying table, Sweden were unbeaten on the way to these finals. They have stepped out of the shadow cast in recent times by Denmark on Scandinavian football.

Olle Nordin's appointment as manager in 1986 was a turning point and, encouraged by the patience traditionally shown to the national coach, he has shaped a side to be respected. In 1988, even though they failed to qualify for the finals of the European Championship, the Swedes were still rated among Europe's better sides. However, to make an impression in Italy, they need to improve up front.

Of special interest to British viewers (particularly those on Merseyside) will be the form of captain Glenn Hysen, Liverpool's strong and tactically outstanding centre-back. Others who promise to catch the eye are Thomas Ravelli, rated one of the best goalkeepers in Europe; Peter Larsson, Hysen's partner in defence; and forward Johnny Ekstrom, who scored the winner against England in a 1986 friendly in Stockholm.

Sweden, absent from the finals of all major tournaments since the 1978 World Championship, reached their one-and-only World Cup Final in 1958, when they were hosts. But Brazil, inspired by 17-year-old Pele, spoiled the party, winning 5 - 2.

Sweden Team Group

Per Larsson

Glenn Hysen

Roger Ljung

Johnny Ekstrom

Roland Nilsson

Thomas Ravelli

VERDICT:

Highly watchable and, remember, they were unbeaten on the road to Italy.

Manager
Mario Zagaol

UNITED ARAB EMIRATES

Group D
Milan Bologna

If the United Arab Emirates so much as win a game in Italy it will certainly be a major shock. They are first-time qualifiers and made it only because, on the final day of the qualifying programme, while UAE were drawing 1 - 1 with South Korea (Asia's other representatives in Italy), China conceded two goals in the last four minutes to lose 2 - 1 to Qatar. That's how close UAE were to missing out on these finals.

Mario Zagalo, three times a winner with Brazil — as a player in 1958 and 1962 and their manager in 1970 — took UAE to the finals, only to find himself sacked! New man Carlos Alberto Parreira will be hoping to add to the miracle UAE have already performed by reaching the 1990 finals. Football is certainly coming of age and there is talk of staging the World Cup in 2002 in Japan, China, Saudi Arabia, South Korea... or could it be in the UAE?

While they do not appear good enough to trouble many opponents in Italy, they are guaranteed to give TV commentators a hard time because they have no less than six players named Mubarak, all unrelated. How about this for a pre-hear of a TV commentator from one of the early group matches in June: "The United Arab Emirates break out of defence... Mubarak passes to Mubarak, now Mubarak through the middle to Mubarak, who plays it out to the wing, where Mubarak crosses for Mubarak No.6 to score. Oh, what a goal — I've never seen one like it!"

UAE TeamGroup

Salim Rabeea

Abdulla Razaqibraham

VERDICT:

Did themselves no favours by sacking Zagalo after he had taken them to the finals.

Manager
Bob Gansler

UNITED STATES OF AMERICA

Group A
Rome Florence

In their anxiety to get to these finals the USA very nearly threw away the chance. Their paltry scoring record caused them to drop points against teams they should have beaten in the Concacaf Group play-offs and meant they had to beat Trinidad & Tobago in their final match, on November 19 last year. The Americans were under intense pressure in Port of Spain, where the whole island was decked out in red, Trinidad's national colour, as the local population willed their country to qualify for the first time. The gates were closed on a capacity crowd of 35,000 five hours before kick-off. Then, on the half-hour, Paul Caligiuri, a Californian from Diamond Bar, who once had a trial with Hamburg, scored America's first goal in 208 minutes' competitive play. It was the winner.

The squad in Italy will be largely based on college graduates. Look out for confident young goalkeeper Tony Meola, who made his debut against El Salvador in September. Coach Bob Gansler is Hungarian-born. The peak of his achievements as a football tutor has been to win the Milwaukee high school tournament — Italy will be something else. From the British viewer's point of view, watching the USA will have a lot more interest now that striker Roy Wegerle has opted to play for them since his £1 million transfer to QPR.

United States Team Group

The Americans are rank outsiders, just as they were in 1950, but that did not prevent them creating one of the biggest upsets in World Cup history when they beat England 1 - 0 in the finals in Brazil. What s that about lightning not striking twice...?

John Harkes

John Stollmeyer

Brian Bliss

VERDICT:

Will learn a lot in Italy - it's a fact finding mission for them on how to stage the next World Cup.

Manager
Washington Tabarez

URUGUAY

Group E
Verona Udine

Twice winners of the World Cup — in the inaugural tournament in 1930 and again in 1950 — Uruguay are the Jekyll and Hyde of football at this level. Moments of breathtaking brilliance are unfortunately often overshadowed by a cynical, sinister approach. Ask Scotland. They were muscled out of the 1986 finals in Mexico, where they could only draw with the South Americans 0 - 0, even though Jose Batista was sent off after 55 seconds. He was the second Uruguayan to be ordered off in the tournament, forcing FIFA to fine them and threaten expulsion from the competition.

Uruguay's journey to Italy has not been easy. Bolivia won their first three games in South America Group One and needed only to draw in Montevideo to qualify. But Uruguay stole top spot on goal difference by winning 2 - 0 and were once again grateful to their Italian-based winger Ruben Sosa, top scorer through the qualifying stages. Uruguay's other big goalscoring hope in Italy is Enzo Francescoli, who disappointed in Mexico, but has since gathered valuable experience of European football alongside Chris Waddle at Olympique Marseille. One thing is certain. Win, lose or draw, Uruguay will be compulsive viewing across the world every time they play in Italy.

Uruguay Team Group

J. Herrera

Perdomo

R. Sousa

Enzo Francescoli

R. Sousa

Enzo Francescoli

VERDICT:

Whether their stay is long or short, you can bet they will be among the tough guys of this World Cup.

Manager
Franz Beckenbauer

WEST GERMANY

Group D
Milan Bologna

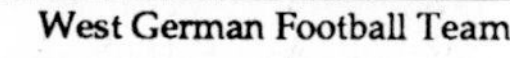
West German Football Team

Cologne, November 15 1989, and fireworks lit up the night sky when West Germany beat Wales side 2 - 1 to qualify from Group 4 in second place, behind Holland.

As Romania had beaten Denmark in Group 1 earlier in the day, the Germans knew they had to beat Wales to be sure of qualifying, and manager Franz Beckenbauer said he would resign if they failed to reach Italy. "West Germany needs to be in the World Cup finals," he explained. And so they are, for the tenth successive time. Although unbeaten, they had a comparatively disappointing qualifying record — three wins in six matches — but the Germans always rise to the occasion in the finals. They have been World Champions twice and runners-up three times, twice in the last three tournaments.

Beckenbauer, sometimes criticised for his style of leadership — most particularly by his former teammate Paul Breitner — has built a side with great potential. The strengths are; powerful running, accuracy of passing and clinical finishing.

Lothar Matthaus, was in superb form in midfield until a knee operation forced him to miss the final qualifying game. West Germany will fervently hope that he is fully fit to take the captain's armband and inspire them again in Italy. Indeed, they are spoilt for choice in midfield with Andreas Brehme and Andy Moller players of experience and distinction. There is also new discovery Thomas Hassler, who was voted Player of the Year for 1988-89 by the captains of the 18 First Division clubs in West Germany.

Bodo Illgner

Hassler is a midfield schemer who has been likened to Gunter Netzer and Wolfgang Overath. A qualified draughtsman, he helped West Germany to a bronze medal in the Seoul Olympics. Big clubs in France and Italy have already tried to tempt Cologne to part with him for millions of Deutschmarks. Hassler could be one of the stars of the World Cup.

Rudi Voller

Pierre Littbarski

Vilfort (Denmark), Andreas Brehme (West Germany)

Jurgen Klinsmann

Olaf Thon

Jurgen Klinsmann

Ricardo Ferri (Italy), Lothar Matthaus (West Germany)

Wolfgang Rolf

VERDICT:

Can never be left out of calculations when the World Cup is held in Europe. Much fancied.

Manager
Ivica Osim

YUGOSLAVIA

Group D
Milan Bologna

Yugoslavia became the first European country to qualify when they beat Scotland 3 - 1 in Zagreb on September 6 of last year. They clinched Group 5 with an unbeaten record — 6 wins, 2 draws, goals 16 - 6 — and dominated it from the beginning, beating France 3 - 2 in Belgrade after securing a valuable 1 - 1 draw at Hampden Park.

The wily Safet Susic was the inspiration behind the victory over France, recalled to the national side at the age of 33 after a four-year absence. Susic made a two-goal international debut in 1977, and has scored three hat-tricks for Yugoslavia. In 1982, he signed a lucrative contract for Paris St Germain and seemed lost to international football. But Ivica Osim, the Yugoslav manager, knew a win over France would be crucial to his team's chances of reaching Italy, so he brought Susic back from exile.

Of the side that beat Scotland to ensure a place in the finals, only three were home-based — the rest scattered all over Europe, with clubs in Italy, Portugal, Switzerland and France. But one of the Slavs' dangermen, Dragan Stojkovic, is very much a 'home' player, starring with Red Star Belgrade.

The Yugoslav domestic game has been blighted in recent years by a series of match-fixing scandals. Getting to the finals in Italy gives Osim and his men the chance to rebuild confidence in their country's football.

Yugoslav World Cup Squad

Haris Skoro

Safet Susic

Dragan Stojkovic

VERDICT:

They are never expected to win World Cups but one of these years they may surprise us.

THE WORLD CUP BOSSES

If the sweepstake at work lands you with some no-hoper like Egypt to win the World Cup, you might have better luck in a lucky dip on how many of the 24 managers or coaches taking their countries to Italy will either be sacked or pack in the job when the Finals are over.

We know of one already. Franz Beckenbauer has decided he will quit after five years as West Germany's manager at the end of Italia '90. He is set to become head of the Federation's marketing division, and his successor is to be his old international team-mate Berti Vogts. Both played in the 1974 World Cup-winning team.

Vogts, who has managed West Germany's youth section, will go to Italy as Franz's assistant, and become No. 1 after Beckenbauer has made his bid to join Mario Zagalo of Brazil in the World Cup records. Zagalo, who led United Arab Emirates to qualification only to find himself sacked, is the only man so far to have played for and later managed World Cup-winning teams.

When the Football Association renewed the contract of England manager Bobby Robson after the 1988 European Championship, they extended it to run a year beyond this World Cup. If England go well in Italy, a further extension is very much on the cards, unless Robson wishes otherwise. We must wait and see.

What we do know is that after the 1986 World Cup in Mexico, no fewer than nine of the 24 competing countries changed their manager.

Those who departed were: Gyorgy Mezey (Hungary) resigned; Jose Torres (Portugal) resigned; Ivan Vutsov (Bulgaria) resigned; Alex Ferguson (Scotland's acting manager) resigned; Rabah Saadane (Algeria) sacked; Antoni Piechniczek (Poland) resigned; Tele Santana (Brazil) resigned; Evaristo de Macedo (Iraq) sacked; and Omar Borras (Uruguay) sacked.

Franz Beckenbauer/West Germany

Bobby Robson/Bryan Robson/England

Azegilio Vicini/Italy

Andy Roxburgh/Scotland

Lazaroni/Brazil

Four years later, these are the managers/coaches preparing to take their national teams to the 1990 World Cup Finals:

Argentina
Carlos Bilardo
Austria
Joseph (Pepi) Hickersberger
Belgium
Guy Thys
Brazil
Sebastiao Lazaroni
Cameroon
Valeri Nepomniaschi
Colombia
Francisco Maturana
Costa Rica
Bora Milutinovic
Czechoslovakia
Josef Venglos
Egypt
Mahmoud El-Gohary
England
Bobby Robson
Holland
Leo Beenhakker
Italy
Azeglio Vicini
Rep. of Ireland
Jack Charlton
Romania
Emerich Jenei
Scotland
Andy Roxburgh
South Korea
Lee Hoe-Taik
Spain
Luis Suarez
Olle Nordin
UAE
Carlos Alberto Parreira
USA
Bob Gansler
Uruguay
Washington Tabarez
Soviet Union
Valery Lobanovsky
West Germany
Franz Beckenbauer
Yugoslavia
Ivica Osim

THE ROAD TO ROME...

...How they qualified

Hosts: **ITALY** *World Cup Holders:* **ARGENTINA**

Europe

Group 1

9.10.88	Greece v Denmark	1-1
19.10.88	Bulgaria v Romania	1-3
2.11.88	Romania v Greece	3-0
2.11.88	Denmark v Bulgaria	1-1
26.4.89	Greece v Romania	0-0
26.4.89	Bulgaria v Denmark	0-2
17.5.89	Romania v Bulgaria	1-0
17.5.89	Denmark v Greece	7-1
11.10.89	Bulgaria v Greece	4-0
11.10.89	Denmark v Romania	3-0
15.11.89	Greece v Bulgaria	1-0
15.11.89	Romania v Denmark	3-1

	P	W	D	L	F	A	Pts
Romania	6	4	1	1	10	5	9
Denmark	6	3	2	1	15	6	8
Greece	6	1	2	3	3	15	4
Bulgaria	6	1	1	4	6	8	3

ROMANIA QUALIFIED Romanian goalscorers: Balinț 2, Camataru 2, Mateut 2, Sabau 2, Hagi 1 (pen), Popescu 1

Group 2

19.10.88	England v Sweden	0-0
19.10.88	Poland v Albania	1-0
5.11.88	Albania v Sweden	1-2
8.3.89	Albania v England	0-2
26.4.89	England v Albania	5-0
7.5.89	Sweden v Poland	2-1
3.6.89	England v Poland	3-0
6.9.89	Sweden v England	0-0
8.10.89	Sweden v Albania	3-1
11.10.89	Poland v England	0-0
25.10.89	Poland v Sweden	0-2
15.11.89	Albania v Poland	1-2

	P	W	D	L	F	A	Pts
Sweden	6	4	2	0	9	3	10
England	6	3	3	0	10	0	9
Poland	6	2	1	3	4	8	5
Albania	6	0	0	6	3	15	0

SWEDEN AND ENGLAND QUALIFIED

Sweden goalscorers: Ekstrom 2, Larsson 2 (1 pen), Engqvist 1, Holmqvist 1, Ingesson 1, Ljung 1, Magnusson 1

England goalscorers: Barnes 2, Beardsley 2, Lineker 2, Gascoigne 1, Robson 1, Waddle 1, Webb 1

Group 3

31.8.88	Iceland v Soviet Union	1-1
12.10.88	Turkey v Iceland	1-1
19.10.88	Soviet Union v Austria	2-0
19.10.88	East Germany v Iceland	2-0
2.11.88	Austria v Turkey	3-2
30.11.88	Turkey v East Germany	3-1
12.4.89	East Germany v Turkey	0-2
26.4.89	Soviet Union v East Germany	3-0
10.5.89	Turkey v Soviet Union	0-1
20.5.89	East Germany v Austria	1-1
31.5.89	Soviet Union v Iceland	1-1
14.6.89	Iceland v Austria	0-0
23.8.89	Austria v Iceland	2-1
6.9.89	Austria v Soviet Union	0-0
6.9.89	Iceland v East Germany	0-3
20.9.89	Iceland v Turkey	2-1
8.10.89	East Germany v Soviet Union	2-1
25.10.89	Turkey v Austria	3-0
15.11.89	Soviet Union v Turkey	2-0
15.11.89	Austria v East Germany	3-0

	P	W	D	L	F	A	Pts
Soviet Union	8	4	3	1	11	4	11
Austria	8	3	3	2	9	9	9
Turkey	8	3	1	4	12	10	7
East Germany	8	3	1	4	9	13	7
Iceland	8	1	4	3	6	11	6

SOVIET UNION AND AUSTRIA QUALIFIED

Soviet Union goalscorers: Litovchenko 3, Dobrovolski 2, Mikhailichenko 2, Protasov 2, Zavarov 1, Own goal 1

Austria goalscorers: Polster 5, Herzog 2, Plelfenberger 1, Zsak 1

Group 4

31.8.88	Finland v West Germany	0-4
14.9.88	Holland v Wales	1-0
19.10.88	Wales v Finland	2-2
19.10.88	West Germany v Holland	0-0
24.4.89	Holland v West Germany	1-1
31.5.89	Wales v West Germany	0-0
31.5.89	Finland v Holland	0-1
6.9.89	Finland v Wales	1-0
4.10.89	West Germany v Finland	6-1
11.10.89	Wales v Holland	1-2
15.11.89	West Germany v Wales	2-1
15.11.89	Holland v Finland	3-0

	P	W	D	L	F	A	Pts
Holland	6	4	2	0	8	2	10
W. Germany	6	3	3	0	13	3	9
Finland	6	1	1	4	4	16	3
Wales	6	0	2	4	4	8	2

HOLLAND AND WEST GERMANY QUALIFIED

Holland goalscorers: Bosman 2, Gullit 1, Kieft 1, E Koeman 1, R Koeman 1 (pen), Rutjes 1, Van Basten 1

West Germany goalscorers: Voller 4, Matthaus 2 (1 pen), Moller 2, Riedle 2, Hassler 1, Klinsmann 1, Littbarski 1

Group 5

14.9.88	Norway v Scotland	1-2
28.9.88	France v Norway	1-0
19.10.88	Scotland v Yugoslavia	1-1
22.10.88	Cyprus v France	1-1
2.11.88	Cyprus v Norway	0-3
19.11.88	Yugoslavia v France	3-2
11.12.88	Yugoslavia v Cyprus	4-0
8.2.89	Cyprus v Scotland	2-3
8.3.89	Scotland v France	2-0
26.4.89	Scotland v Cyprus	2-1
29.4.89	France v Yugoslavia	0-0
21.5.89	Norway v Cyprus	3-1

Peter Shilton/England

Peter Beardsley/England

14.6.89	Norway v Yugoslavia	1-2
5.9.89	Norway v France	1-1
6.9.89	Yugoslavia v Scotland	3-1
11.10.89	Yugoslavia v Norway	1-0
11.10.89	France v Scotland	3-0
28.10.89	Cyprus v Yugoslavia	1-2
15.11.89	Scotland v Norway	1-1
18.11.89	France v Cyprus	2-0

	P	W	D	L	F	A	Pts
Yugoslavia	8	6	2	0	16	6	14
Scotland	8	4	2	2	12	12	10
France	8	3	3	2	10	7	9
Norway	8	2	2	4	10	9	6
Cyprus	8	0	1	7	6	20	1

YUGOSLAVIA AND SCOTLAND QUALIFIED.
Yugoslavia goalscorers: Savicevic 3, Stojkovic 3, Hadzibegic 2 (2 pens), Katenac 2, Vujovic 2, Pancev 1, Spasic 1, Susic 1, Own goal 1
Scotland goalscorers: Johnston 6, Gough 2, McCoist 2, Durie 1, McStay 1

Group 6

21.5.88	N Ireland v Malta	3-0
14.9.88	N Ireland v Rep of Ireland	0-0
19.10.88	Hungary v N Ireland	1-0
16.11.88	Spain v Rep of Ireland	2-0
11.12.88	Malta v Hungary	2-2
21.12.88	Spain v N Ireland	4-0
22.1.89	Malta v Spain	0-2
8.2.89	N Ireland v Spain	0-2
8.3.89	Hungary v Rep of Ireland	0-0
22.3.89	Spain v Malta	4-0
12.4.89	Hungary v Malta	1-1
26.4.89	Malta v N Ireland	0-2
26.4.89	Rep of Ireland v Spain	1-0
28.5.89	Rep of Ireland v Malta	2-0
4.6.89	Rep of Ireland v Hungary	2-0
6.9.89	N Ireland v Hungary	1-2
11.10.89	Hungary v Spain	2-2
11.10.89	Rep of Ireland v N Ireland	3-0
15.11.89	Spain v Hungary	4-0
15.11.89	Malta v Rep of Ireland	0-2

	P	W	D	L	F	A	Pts
Spain	8	6	1	1	20	3	13
Rep of Ireland	8	5	2	1	10	2	12
Hungary	8	2	4	2	8	12	8
N Ireland	8	2	1	5	6	12	5
Malta	8	0	2	6	3	18	2

SPAIN AND REPUBLIC OF IRELAND QUALIFIED
Spain goalscorers: Manolo 5, Michel 4 (3 pens), Butragueno 3, Adrinua 1, Beguiristain 1, Fernando 1, Juanito 1, Salinas 1, Own goals 3
Republic of Ireland goalscorers: Aldridge 2 (1 pen), Cascarino 2, Houghton 2, McGrath 1, Moran 1, Whelan 1, Own goal 1

Group 7

1.9.88	Luxembourg v Switzerland	1-4
19.10.88	Luxembourg v C'slovakia	0-2
19.10.88	Belgium v Switzerland	1-0
16.11.88	C'slovakia v Belgium	0-0
16.11.88	Portugal v Luxembourg	1-0
15.2.89	Portugal v Belgium	1-1
26.4.89	Portugal v Switzerland	3-1
30.4.89	Belgium v C'slovakia	2-1
19.5.89	C'slovakia v Luxembourg	4-0
1.6.89	Luxembourg v Belgium	0-5
7.6.89	Switzerland v C'slovakia	0-1
6.9.89	Belgium v Portugal	3-0
20.9.89	Switzerland v Portugal	1-2
6.10.89	C'slovakia v Portugal	2-1
11.10.89	Luxembourg v Portugal	0-3
11.10.89	Switzerland v Belgium	2-2
25.10.89	C'slovakia v Switzerland	3-0
25.10.89	Belgium v Luxembourg	1-1
15.11.89	Portugal v C'slovakia	0-0
15.11.89	Switzerland v Luxembourg	2-1

	P	W	D	L	F	A	Pts
Belgium	8	4	4	0	15	5	12
Czechoslovakia	8	5	2	1	13	3	12
Portugal	8	4	2	2	11	8	10
Switzerland	8	2	1	5	10	14	5
Luxembourg	8	0	1	7	3	22	1

BELGIUM AND CZECHOSLOVAKIA QUALIFIED
Belgium goalscorers: Van der Linden 5, Vervoort 4, Degryse 3, Ceulemans 1, Versavel 1, Own goal 1
Czechoslovakia goalscorers: Bilek 4 (1 pen), Skuhravy 4, Chovanec 1, Griga 1, Hasek 1, Luhovy 1, Moravcik 1
England and West Germany also qualified from Europe as best-record runners-up in the four-country groups (1, 2 and 4).

South America

Group 1

20.8.89	Bolivia v Peru	2-1
27.8.89	Peru v Uruguay	0-2
3.9.89	Bolivia v Uruguay	2-1
10.9.89	Peru v Bolivia	1-2
17.9.89	Uruguay v Bolivia	2-0
24.9.89	Uruguay v Peru	2-0

	P	W	D	L	F	A	Pts
Uruguay	4	3	0	1	7	2	6
Bolivia	4	3	0	1	6	5	6
Peru	4	0	0	4	2	8	0

URUGUAY QUALIFIED

Uruguay goalscorers: Sosa 4, Alzamendi 2, Francescoli 1

Group 2

20.8.89	Colombia v Ecuador	2-0
27.8.89	Paraguay v Colombia	2-1
3.9.89	Ecuador v Colombia	0-0
10.9.89	Paraguay v Ecuador	2-1
24.9.89	Colombia v Paraguay	2-1
1.10.89	Ecuador v Peru	3-1

	P	W	D	L	F	A	Pts
Colombia	4	2	1	1	5	3	5
Paraguay	4	2	0	2	6	7	4
Ecuador	4	1	1	2	4	5	3

COLOMBIA QUALIFIED to play Israel (Oceania Group winners) for a place in the finals and won 1-0 on aggregate (1-0 at home, 0-0 away).

Colombia goalscorers: Iguaran 4, Hernandez 1, Uzurriaga 1

Group 3

30.7.89	Venezuela v Brazil	1-3
6.8.89	Venezuela v Chile	1-3
13.8.89	Chile v Brazil	1-1
20.8.89	Brazil v Venezuela	6-0
27.8.89	Chile v Venezuela	5-0
3.9.89	Brazil v Chile	2-0

	P	W	D	L	F	A	Pts
Brazil	4	3	1	0	12	2	7
Chile	4	2	1	1	9	4	5
Venezuela	4	0	0	4	2	17	0

BRAZIL QUALIFIED

Brazil goalscorers: Careca 5, Bebeto 2, Branco 1, Romario 1, Silas 1, Own goals 2

Diego Maradona / Argentina

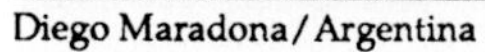

Diego Maradona / Argentina

Diego Maradona / Argentina

Africa

Group B

ROUND 2

6.1.89	Egypt v Liberia	2-0
7.1.89	Kenya v Malawi	1-1
21.1.89	Malawi v Egypt	1-1
22.1.89	Liberia v Kenya	0-0
10.6.89	Kenya v Egypt	0-0
11.6.89	Liberia v Malawi	1-0
24.6.89	Malawi v Kenya	1-0
25.6.89	Liberia v Egypt	1-0
11.8.89	Egypt v Malawi	1-0
12.8.89	Kenya v Liberia	1-0
25.8.89	Egypt v Kenya	2-0
26.8.89	Malawi v Liberia	0-0

	P	W	D	L	F	A	Pts
Egypt	6	3	2	1	6	2	8
Liberia	6	2	2	2	2	3	6
Malawi	6	1	3	2	3	4	5
Kenya	6	1	3	2	2	4	5

Group C

7.1.89	Nigeria v Gabon	1-0
8.1.89	Cameroon v Angola	1-1
22.1.89	Gabon v Cameroon	1-3
22.1.89	Angola v Nigeria	2-2
10.6.89	Nigeria v Cameroon	2-0
10.6.89	Angola v Gabon	2-0
25.6.89	Angola v Cameroon	1-2
25.6.89	Gabon v Nigeria	2-1
12.8.89	Nigeria v Angola	1-0
13.8.89	Cameroon v Gabon	2-1
27.8.89	Cameroon v Nigeria	1-0
27.8.89	Gabon v Angola	1-0

	P	W	D	L	F	A	Pts
Cameroon	6	4	1	1	9	6	9
Nigeria	6	3	1	2	7	5	7
Angola	6	1	2	3	6	7	4
Gabon	6	2	0	4	5	9	4

ROUND 3

8.10.89	Algeria v Egypt	0-0
8.10.89	Cameroon v Tunisia	2-0
17.11.89	Egypt v Algeria	1-0
19.11.89	Tunisia v Cameroon	0-1

EGYPT (1-0 AGG) AND CAMEROON (3-0 AGG) QUALIFY (neither country played in Round 1 of the Africa qualifying tournament)

Egypt goalscorers: Abder Rassoul 3, Ibrahim Hassan 2, Mayhaud 1, Rumudun 1

Cameroon goalscorers: Oman-Biyik 5, M'Bouh 2, Bonavemure 1, Kana-Biyik 1, Kunde 1, M'Fede 1, Ojoukep 1

Asia

Group 4

East Asia

Following matches all played in South Korea:

23.5.89	Malaysia v Nepal	2-0
23.5.89	Singapore v South Korea	0-3
25.5.89	Malaysia v Singapore	1-0
25.5.89	Nepal v South Korea	0-9
27.5.89	Singapore v Nepal	3-0
27.5.89	South Korea v Malaysia	3-0

Following matches all played in Singapore:

3.6.89	Singapore v Malaysia	2-2
3.6.89	South Korea v Nepal	4-0
5.6.89	Malaysia v South Korea	0-3
5.6.89	Nepal v Singapore	0-7
7.6.89	Singapore v South Korea	0-3
7.6.89	Malaysia v Nepal	3-0

	P	W	D	L	F	A	Pts
South Korea	6	6	0	0	25	0	12
Malaysia	6	3	1	2	8	8	7
Singapore	6	2	1	3	12	9	5
Nepal	6	0	0	6	0	28	0

Group 3

West Asia

6.1.89	Pakistan v Kuwait	0-1
13.1.89	Kuwait v UAE	3-2
20.1.89	UAE v Pakistan	5-0
27.1.89	Kuwait v Pakistan	2-0
3.2.89	UAE v Kuwait	1-0
10.2.89	Pakistan v UAE	1-4

	P	W	D	L	F	A	Pts
UAE	4	3	0	1	12	4	6
Kuwait	4	3	0	1	6	3	6
Pakistan	4	0	0	4	1	2	0

Of the six initial Asian qualifying groups we have featured only those two from which the eventual qualifiers emerged.

Play-off section — ROUND 2

Following matches played in Singapore, except for UAE v South Korea (in Kuala Lumpur) and Saudi Arabia v North Korea (in Kuanton):

12.10.89	UAE v North Korea	0-0
12.10.89	China v Saudi Arabia	2-1
13.10.89	South Korea v Qatar	0-0
16.10.89	Qatar v Saudi Arabia	1-1
16.10.89	South Korea v North Korea	1-0
17.10.89	China v UAE	1-2
20.10.89	China v South Korea	0-1
20.10.89	North Korea v Qatar	2-0
21.10.89	Saudi Arabia v UAE	0-0
24.10.89	UAE v Qatar	1-1
24.10.89	North Korea v China	0-1
25.10.89	Saudi Arabia v South Korea	0-2
28.10.89	UAE v South Korea	1-1
28.10.89	Saudi Arabia v North Korea	2-0
28.10.89	Qatar v China	2-1

	P	W	D	L	F	A	Pts
South Korea	5	3	2	0	5	1	8
UAE	5	1	4	0	4	3	6
Qatar	5	1	3	1	4	5	5
China	5	2	0	3	5	6	4
Saudi Arabia	5	1	2	2	4	5	4
North Korea	5	1	1	3	2	4	3

SOUTH KOREA AND UNITED ARAB EMIRATES QUALIFIED

South Korea goalscorers: Seon-Hong 7, Soo Jin 4, Yong Se 4, Hwangbo-Kwan 2, Min Kook 2, Soon Ho 2, Tae Ho 2, Hwak Jong 1, Hwang Bo 1, Joo-Sung 1, Kyung Hoon 1, Sang Kook 1, Yong Hwan 1, Yong Jin 1

UAE goalscorers: Ibrahim 3, Al Taliani 2, Bakheet 2, Ismail 2, Mubarak 2, Talyani 2, Aziz 1, Mohammed 1, Rahman 1

North & Central America

ROUND 1

17.7.88	Costa Rica v Panama	1-1
31.7.88	Panama v Costa Rica	0-2

Costa Rica won 3-1 on aggregate

ROUND 2

1.10.88	N'lands Antilles v El Salvador	0-1
16.10.88	El Salvador v N'lands Antilles	5-0

El Salvador won 6-0 on aggregate

30.10.88	T'dad & Tobago v Honduras	0-0
13.11.88	Honduras v T'dad & Tobago	1-1

Trinidad & Tobago won on away goals

24.7.88	Jamaica v United States	0-0
13.8.88	United States v Jamaica	5-1

United States won 5-1 on aggregate

9.10.88	Guatemala v Canada	1-0
15.10.88	Canada v Guatemala	3-2

Guatemala won on away goals
Costa Rica walked over v Mexico

ROUND 3

19.3.89	Guatemala v Costa Rica	1-0
2.4.89	Costa Rica v Guatemala	2-1
16.4.89	Costa Rica v USA	1-0
30.4.89	USA v Costa Rica	1-0
13.5.89	USA v T'dad & Tobago	1-1
28.5.89	T'dad & Tobago v Costa Rica	1-1
11.6.89	Costa Rica v T'dad & Tobago	1-0
17.6.89	United States v Guatemala	2-1
25.6.89	El Salvador v Costa Rica	2-4
16.7.89	Cost Rica v El Salvador	1-0
30.7.89	T'dad & Tobago v El Salvador	2-0
13.8.89	El Salvador v T'dad & Tobago	0-0
20.8.89	Guatemala v T'dad & Tobago	0-1
3.9.89	T'dad & Tobago v Guatemala	2-1
17.9.89	El Salvador v USA	0-1
8.10.89	Guatemala v USA	0-0
5.11.89	USA v El Salvador	0-0
19.11.89	T'dad & Tobago v USA	0-1
19.11.89	Guatemala v El Salvador	OFF
26.11.89	El Salvador v Guatemala	OFF

Final two fixtures called off because of hostilities in El Salvador

	P	W	D	L	F	A	Pts
Costa Rica	8	5	1	2	10	6	11
Unites States	8	4	3	1	6	3	11
T'dad & Tobago	8	3	3	2	7	5	9
Guatemala	6	1	1	4	4	7	3
El Salvador	6	0	2	4	2	8	2

COSTA RICA AND UNITED STATES QUALIFIED

Costa Rica goalscorers: Cayasso 3, Flores 3, Coronado 2, Fernandez 1, Hidalgo 1, Jara 1, Medford 1, Roden 1

United States goalscorers: Klopas 2, Perez 2, Bliss 1, Caligiuri 1, Eichmann 1, Krumpe 1, Murray 1, Ramos 1, Trittschuh 1

THE HISTORY OF THE CUP

URUGUAY 1930

WINNERS Uruguay RUNNERS-UP Argentina THIRD USA

Other countries taking part Belgium, Bolivia, Brazil, Chile, France, Mexico, Paraguay, Peru, Romania, Yugoslavia
Total entries 13
Venue All matches played in Montevideo **Top scorer** Stabile (Argentina) 8 goals
Final Uruguay 4 (Dorado, Cea, Iriarte, Castro), Argentina 2 (Peucelle, Stabile)
Half-time Uruguay 1, Argentina 2 **Attendance** 90,000
Uruguay Ballesteros, Nasazzi, Mascheroni, Andrade, Fernandez,
Gestido, Dorado, Scarone, Castro, Cea, Iriarte
Argentina Botasso, Della Torre, Paternoster, Evaristo J, Monti, Suarez, Peucelle, Varallo, Stabile, Ferreira, Evaristo M

The World Cup was the brainchild of Jules Rimet, a French lawyer, and came into being in 1930. Rimet, who became president of FIFA — the governing body of international football — in 1920, himself donated a handsome trophy. The Jules Rimet Cup, as it became known, was made of solid gold and weighed nine pounds, though standing only a foot high.

The first tournament, played exclusively in Montevideo, the capital of Uruguay, was not truly representative, however. Teams from Great Britain were not affiliated to FIFA at that time and did not compete until 1950. The hosts were generous. They offered to pay the expenses of the competing teams. But travel was more difficult then and only 13 countries, including four from Europe, took part.

Yugoslavia did the best among the Europeans, reaching the semi-finals, in which they were beaten 6-1 by Argentina. Boatloads of Argentines crossed the River Plate for the first World Cup Final between Argentina and Uruguay, on July 30, 1930. The home team, aided by two months' intensive training and a partisan crowd of 90,000, recovered from a half-time deficit to win 4-2.

In Uruguay, a public holiday was announced. In Buenos Aires, angry Argentines stoned the Uruguayan consulate.

ITALY 1934

WINNERS Italy RUNNERS-UP Czechoslovakia THIRD Germany

Other countries in finals Argentina, Austria, Belgium, Brazil, Egypt, France, Holland, Hungary, Rumania, Spain, Sweden, Switzerland, USA **Total entries** 29 (16 qualifiers)
Venues Rome, Naples, Milan, Turin, Florence, Bologna, Genoa, Trieste **Top scorers** Schiavio (Italy), Nejedly (Czechoslovakia), Conen (Germany), each 4 goals
Final (Rome) Italy 2 (Orsi, Schiavio), Czechoslovakia 1 (Puc). **after extra time.**
Half-time 0 -1. Score after 90 minutes: 1-1 **Attendance** 50,000
Italy Combi, Montezeglio, Allemandi, Ferraris, Monti, Bertolini, Guaita, Meazza, Schiavio, Ferrari, Orsi
Czechoslovakia Planicka, Zenisek, Ctyroky, Kostalek, Cambal, Krcil, Junek, Svoboda, Sobotka, Nejedly, Puc

The holders Uruguay did not defend their title in Italy because so many countries had stayed away from their event, four years earlier.

For the first time, there was a qualifying competition and the 16 nations who reached the finals came from an even wider area. Europe was well represented with Austria, Czechoslovakia, Egypt and Switzerland among the new faces in the finals. The tournament was run on a knock-out basis which meant that Brazil and Argentina, beaten in the first round, had travelled 8,000 miles to play one match. Italy, coached by the astute authoritarian Vittorio Pozzo, conceded only two goals in reaching the Final. Pozzo, himself no Fascist, cleverly used the mood of the time — Mussolini was in power — to rally his players with patriotic rhetoric.

The plan looked to have gone wrong when the Czechs took the lead in with 20 minutes remaining in the Final. They also hit the post, but Italy managed to force extra-time when Argentine-born Raimondo Orsi scored late in the game with a cruelly curling shot.

Italy clinched the title when Schiavio, the joint scorer in the tournament, scored the winner in the extra period.

1990 World Cup Stadium, Turin

FRANCE 1938

WINNERS Italy RUNNERS-UP Hungary THIRD Brazil

Other countries in finals Belgium, Cuba, Czechoslovakia, Dutch East Indies, France, Germany, Holland, Norway, Poland, Romania, Sweden, Switzerland **Total entries** 25 (15 qualifiers)
Venues Paris, Marseilles, Bordeaux, Lille, Antibes, Strasbourg, Le Havre, Reims, Toulouse **Top scorer** Leonidas (Brazil) 8 goals
Final (Paris) Italy 4 (Colaussi 2, Piola 2), Hungary 2 (Titkos, Sarosi)
Half-time 3-1 **Attendance** 45,000
Italy Olivieri, Foni, Rava, Serantoni, Andreolo, Locatelli, Biavati, Meazza, Piloa, Ferrari, Colaussi
Hungary Szabo, Polgar, Biro, Szalay, Szucs, Lazar, Sas, Vincze, Sarosi, Szengeller, Titkos

The 1938 tournament, unlike the modern tradition, did not return to Latin America four years after being held in Europe. Argentina wanted to hold the competition and pulled out when they were refused. Football fans in Argentina rioted outside the football federation's offices in Buenos Aires.

This World Cup was played under the shadow of war. German troops had already invaded the Rhineland. Austria qualified for the finals but their country was overrun and they had to withdraw.

France could not maintain the pattern of home victories. They were beaten 3-1 in the second round by Italy, still coached by Pozzo. The tournament was again played on a knock-out basis, which meant that some of the less developed footballing nations, such as the the Dutch East Indies, made an early exit.

There was a battle of another kind when Brazil met Czechoslovakia in the second round. Three players were sent off and there were two broken limbs. The game was drawn and Brazil won a much more peaceful replay.

Pozzo and his men were unstoppable, however, and beat Hungary 4 - 2 in the Final to retain the Cup.He said: "We left aside all flourishes, anything resembling ballet". There was not another World Cup tournament for 12 years because of the Second World War, however, the trophy survived the war years, hidden under the bed of the Italian Football Association's vice-president.

BRAZIL 1950

WINNERS Uruguay RUNNERS-UP Brazil THIRD Sweden

Other countries in finals Bolivia, Chile, England, Italy, Mexico, Paraguay, Spain, Switzerland, USA, Yugoslavia
Total entries 29 (13 qualifiers)
Venues Rio de Janeiro, Sao Paulo, Recife, Curitiba, Belo Horizonte, Porto Alegre **Top scorer** Ademir (Brazil) 7 goals
Deciding Match (Rio de Janeiro) Uruguay 2 (Schiaffino, Ghiggia), Brazil 1 (Friaca)
(For the only time, the World Cup was decided on a Final Pool system, in which the winners of the four qualifying groups met in a six-match series. So, unlike previous and subsequent tournaments, there was no official Final as such, but Uruguay v Brazil was the deciding final match in the Final Pool.) **Half-time** 0-0 **Attendance** 200,000
Uruguay Maspoli, Gonzales, Tejera, Gambetta, Varela, Andrade, Ghiggia, Perez, Miguez, Schiaffino, Moran
Brazil Barbosa, Augusto, Juvenal, Bauer, Danilo, Bigode, Griaca, Zizinho, Ademir, Jair, Chico

This was the World Cup which saw England compete for the first time. The British Associations had re-entered FIFA and were now eligible, but only England entered. They did not make a distinguished debut. England beat Chile in their opening pool game in Rio, and then travelled to the cooler Belo Horizonte to take on the unfancied United States team. Stanley Matthews was rested — England still had Billy Wright, Tom Finney and Stan Mortensen in the team. But it was a Haitian-born centre forward called Larry Gaetjens who grabbed the headlines. His 30th minute header earned a sensational victory for the USA. England never recovered their poise and were beaten by Spain in their next game to condemn them to an embarrassing exit.

The host nation Brazil had magnificent wins against Sweden (7-1) and Spain (6-1) in the final pool and needed only to draw with Uruguay in their last match to become World Champions. An incredible crowd of 200,000, a world record attendance, filled the giant Maracana Stadium in Rio.

Brazil scored two minutes after half-time but Uruguay, whose defence had held out magnificently under almost constant attack in the first period, wore them down. Two goals, by Schiaffino and Ghiggia, broke the hearts of the Brazilians and Uruguay maintaining their unbeaten record in the World Cup, were crowned champions for the second time.

1990 World Cup Stadium, Genoa

SWITZERLAND 1954

WINNERS West Germany RUNNERS-UP Hungary
THIRD Austria

Other countries in finals Belgium, Brazil, Czechoslovakia, England, France, Italy, Korea, Mexico, Scotland, Switzerland, Turkey, Uruguay, Yugoslavia **Total entries** 35 (16 qualifiers)
Venues Berne, Zurich, Lausanne, Basle, Geneva, Lugano
Top scorer Kocsis (Hungary) 11 goals
Final (Berne): West Germany 3 (Morlock, Rahn 2), Hungary 2 (Puskas, Czibor)
Half-time 2-2 **Attendance** 60,000
West Germany Turek, Posipal, Kohlmeyer, Eckel, Liebrich, Mai, Rahn, Morlock, Walter O, Walter F, Schaefer
Hungary Grosics, Buzansky, Lantos, Boszik, Lorant, Zakarias, Czibor, Kocsis, Hidegkuti, Puskas, Toth

The 1954 finals were the first to be televised and where Hungary, with Puskas and much of the side which had humbled England at Wembley months earlier, were expected to be unbeatable.

Britain was represented for the first time by both England and Scotland. Scotland were beaten by Austria and Czechoslovakia but England reached the quarter-finals, where they were beaten 4-2 by Uruguay, despite a virtuoso performance by Stanley Matthews.

The Hungarians eased through their group games, beating Korea 9-0 and West Germany 8-3. They went through to the Final by beating Brazil 4-2 in the quarter-finals and Uruguay by the same score a round later. This was the first defeat the Uruguayans had ever suffered in World Cup competition. The West Germans had been crafty. They purposely fielded a weak team against Hungary, because they were sure they could still qualify for the quarter-finals by beating Turkey and thereby secure an easier passage to the Final. The plan worked. West Germany thrashed Turkey 7-2 and then beat Yugoslavia and Austria.

In the Final, Hungary went 2-0 ahead in eight minutes through Puskas and Czibor but the determined Germans were level within 10 minutes. Hungary had little luck in the second half, hitting the bar, the post and having a goal disallowed. The Germans scored the winner five minutes from the end when Rahn collected his second goal and so won their first World Cup.

SWEDEN 1958

WINNERS Brazil RUNNERS-UP Sweden THIRD France

Other countries in finals Argentina, Austria, Czechoslovakia, England, Hungary, Mexico, Northern Ireland, Paraguay, Soviet Union, Scotland, Wales, West Germany, Yugoslavia
Total entries 47 (16 qualifiers)
Venues Stockholm, Gothenburg, Malmo, Norrkoping, Boras, Sandviken, Eskilstuna, Cerebro, Vasteras, Halsingborg, Halmstad
Top scorer Fontaine (France) 13 goals
Final (Stockholm) Brazil 5 (Vava 2, Pele 2, Zagalo), Sweden 2 (Liedholm, Simonsson)
Half-time 2-1 **Attendance** 50,000
Brazil Gilmar, Santos D, Santos N, Zio, Bellini, Orlando, Garrincha, Didi, Vava, Pele, Zagalo
Sweden Svensson, Bergmark, Axbom, Boerjesson, Gustavsson, Parling, Hamrin, Gren, Simonsson, Liedholm, Skoglund

Imagine a World Cup today with a full hand of all four home countries competing — this was the situation in 1958 when, for the first and only time, the Home Countries were fully represented. England held Brazil to a 0-0 draw but were eliminated after losing to the Soviet Union in a play-off while Scotland collected one point out of six. Northern Ireland and Wales did the best, reaching the quarter-finals. But the stars of the tournament were the Brazilians, and particularly a 17-year-old called Pele. Brazil played a 4-2-4 system in which creative midfield players Didi and Zito provided the passes which Pele and fellow striker Vava converted.

The Brazilians scored six goals without reply until the semi-finals, in which they beat France 5-2. France had the consolation of having the tournament's top scorer in 13 goal Fontaine.

Again the host nation reached the final, where their opponents were Brazil. Sweden delighted the crowd by taking the lead but Brazil then produced one of the truly great displays of football. Vava and Pele, with a brilliant volley and a header, scored twice each and Brazil over-ran the Swedes 5-2, the biggest ever World Cup victory.

Sweden, in their first Final, played so well that King Gustav Adolf, who was watching from the Royal Box, awarded them the Order of Merit. Brazil won the hearts and minds of the most partisan Swedish supporters and they were cheered to their first World Cup win.

1990 World Cup Rome Olympic Stadium

1990 World Cup Stadium, Bari

CHILE 1962

WINNERS Brazil RUNNERS-UP Czechoslovakia THIRD Chile

Other countries in finals Argentina, Bulgaria, Colombia, England, Hungary, Italy, Mexico, Soviet Union, Spain, Switzerland, Uruguay, West Germany, Yugoslavia
Total entries 53 (16 qualifiers)
Venues Santiago, Vina del Mar, Rancagua, Arica.
Top scorers Garrincha (Brazil), Vava (Brazil), Sanchez (Chile), Albert (Hungary), Ivanov (Russia), Jerkovic (Yugoslavia) each 4 goals.
Final (Santiago) Brazil 3 (Amarildo, Zito, Vava), Czechoslovakia 1 (Masopust)
Half-time 1-1 **Attendance** 69,000
Brazil Gilmar, Santos D, Mauro, Zozimo, Santos N, Zito, Didi, Garrincha, Vava, Amarildo, Zagalo
Czechoslovakia Schroiff, Tichy, Novak, Pluskaj, Popluhar, Masopust, Pospichal, Scherer, Kvasniak, Kadraba, Jelinek

Back in Latin America, the seventh World Cup produced a competition almost as poor as the country which staged it, although Chile had made tremendous and successful efforts to build new stadia and provide the right setting. Unfortunately, in contrast to Sweden, defences dominated. There were only 89 goals, compared with 126 in 1958 and 140 in 1954. It was the least memorable contest for the Jules Rimet Cup since it became a truly world-wide tournament.

The dark side of football had cast a shadow earlier in the tournament, during a violent group match between Chile and Italy. Two Italians, Ferrini and David, were sent off, while their team-mates had to be restrained by police during a 'confrontation' won 2-0 by the hosts.

England, Britain's lone representatives, went out 3-1 to Brazil, the eventual winners, in the quarter-finals. The English could find no answer to Garrincha at Vina del Mar. He scored the first goal, made the second for Vava and hit a swerving free-kick for Brazil's third.

Pele was lost to Brazil through injury early in the competition, but although now an ageing side and far less impressive than four years previously, they retained the trophy, beating Czechoslovakia in the Final 3-1 after being a goal down.

ENGLAND 1966

WINNERS England RUNNERS-UP West Germany THIRD Portugal

Other countries in finals Argentina, Brazil, Bulgaria, Chile, France, Hungary, Italy, Mexico, North Korea, Soviet Union, Spain, Switzerland, Uruguay **Total entries** 53 (16 qualifiers)
Venues London (Wembley and White City), Sheffield (Hillsborough), Liverpool (Goodison Park), Sunderland, Middlesbrough, Manchester (Old Trafford), Birmingham (Villa Park) **Top scorer** Eusebio (Portugal) 9 goals
Final (Wembley) England 4 (Hurst 3, Peters), West Germany 2 (Haller, Weber) **after extra time**
Half-time 1-1. Score after 90 minutes: 2-2 Attendance 100,000
England Banks, Cohen, Wilson, Stiles, Charlton J, Moore, Ball, Hurst, Hunt, Charlton R, Peters
West Germany Tilkowski, Hottges, Schnellinger, Beckenbauer, Schulz, Weber, Haller, Held, Seeler, Overath, Emmerich

Four months before they staged the World Cup, England literally lost it. The solid gold cup vanished in a daring daylight theft from a padlocked cabinet while on display at a stamp exhibition in Westminster. Seven days later a mongrel dog named Pickles sniffed at a parcel lying under a bush in Upper Norwood in South London — and the World Cup was found intact. England then proceeded to have their finest hour and became the first host nation to win the World Cup since Italy in 1934.

The 1966 World Cup was also memorable for the stirring deeds of North Korea. A sensational 1-0 win against Italy took them into the quarter-finals, at which stage they lost 5-3 to Portugal.

The England manger Alf Ramsey, subsequently knighted, was the undisputed architect of England's success. He ignored all the jibes about 'wingless wonders' and fashioned a team based on the class of Gordon Banks in goal, Bobby Moore in defence, Bobby Charlton in attack and the dramatic goalscoring of Geoff Hurst. Hurst clinched England's famous 4-2 victory at Wembley with the only hat-trick in a World Cup final. The game went into extra time for only the second time in history and the first since 1934. A crucial decision went their way over the third goal, when Hurst's shot bounced down from the crossbar. The Russian linesman confirmed that the ball was over the line, but none of the cameras present got a clear picture to prove it.

MEXICO 1970

WINNERS Brazil RUNNERS-UP Italy THIRD West Germany

Other countries in finals Belgium, Bulgaria, Czechoslovakia, El Salvador, England, Israel, Mexico, Morocco, Peru, Romania, Soviet Union, Sweden, Uruguay
Total entries 68 (16 qualifiers)
Venues Mexico City, Guadalajara, Leon, Puebla, Toluca
Top scorer Muller (West Germany) 10 goals
Final (Mexico City) Brazil 4 (Pele, Gerson, Jairzinho, Carlos Alberto), Italy 1 (Boninsegna)
Half-time 1-1 **Attendance** 107,000
Brazil Felix, Carlos Alberto, Brito, Piazza, Everaldo, Clodoalda, Gerson, Jairzinho, Tostao, Pele, Rivelino
Italy Albertosi, Burgnich, Facchetti, Cera, Rosato, Bertini (Juliano), Domenghini, De Sisti, Mazzola, Boninsegna (Rivera), Riva

The memorable 1970 tournament climaxed with Brazil's mesmerising 4-1 victory in the Final against Italy was a football masterpiece. By winning all six matches they were required to play, Brazil worthily became the first country to take the World Cup three times and, in doing so, won the Jules Rimet trophy outright.

England progressed to the quarter-finals, but disaster was to follow in a re-match of the '66 Final with West Germany in Leon. For an hour, England played splendidly and when Martin Peters added to Alan Mullery's first-half goal directly after the interval, a 2-0 lead looked unassailable. But Beckenbauer reduced the arrears with a shot that flashed under replacement goalkeeper Peter Bonetti and Germany pulled level when Seeler scored with a late header.

So, the sides went into extra time at 2-2. The Germans emerged triumphant, winning 3-2 thanks to Muller.

Pele, kicked out of the two previous World Cups, was at his spectacular best in his fourth tournament. He opened the scoring in the Final and tormented the Italians throughout. It mattered not that Brazil had a suspect defence; their game was based on creation in midfield and a flair for all-out attack. Brazil were responsible for 19 of the 95 goals scored in the 32-match programme.

Jairzinho was a constant threat. He scored Brazil's third goal in the Final and became the first player to score in every game in the finals. His goal had beaten England, when Brazil met the World Cup holders in a Guadalajara group match early in the tournament.

1990 World Cup Stadium, Cagliari

WEST GERMANY 1974

WINNERS West Germany RUNNERS-UP Holland THIRD Poland

Other countries in finals Argentina, Australia, Brazil, Bulgaria, Chile, East Germany, Haiti, Italy, Scotland, Sweden, Uruguay, Yugoslavia, Zaire **Total entries** 98 (16 qualifiers)
Venues Berlin, Hamburg, Frankfurt, Dortmund, Gelsenkirchen, Hanover, Dusseldorf, Stuttgart, Munich
Top scorer Lato (Poland) 7 goals
Final (Munich) West Germany 2 (Breitner — penalty, Muller), Holland 1 (Neeskens — penalty)
Half-time 2-1 **Attendance** 77,833
West Germany Maier, Vogts, Schwarzenbeck, Beckenbauer, Breitner, Bonhof, Hoeness, Overath, Grabowski, Muller, Holzenbein
Holland Jongbloed, Suurbier, Rijsbergen (De Jong), Hann, Krol, Jansen, Van Hanegem, Neeskens, Rep, Cruyff, Resenbrink (Van der Kerkhof R)

With Brazil winning the old Jules Rimet Trophy outright in 1970 a new FIFA trophy appeared, as did a new format, for the tenth World Cup. Pele had retired, but Johan Cruyff and Holland's 'total football' had arrived. However, Helmut Schoen's West Germany became the fourth host nation to win the title, coming from behind to beat Holland 2-1. They were also the first country to hold the World and European Championships simultaneously.

Scotland, Britain's sole representatives, paid the price for their lack of goals when they were eliminated from group two on goal difference without losing a match. They were the only country to finish the tournament unbeaten.

With the quarter-finals and semi-finals discontinued, the Dutch and Germans qualified for the Final with 100 per cent records from the two groups into which the last eight countries were divided. The 77,000 at the Final in Munich did not have to wait long for the drama to unfold. Straight from the kick-off, and before even one German had touched the ball, Cruyff was brought down by Hoeness. English referee Jack Taylor bravely awarded the first penalty in the history of World Cup Finals, and Neeskens scored the fastest Final goal in history.

Despite their skill and fluency, Holland's lead was short-lived. Breitner equalised with another penalty in the 25th minute and Muller scored the winner two minutes before half-time. Individual style within the framework of the team had made Holland the most attractive team in the tournament under the managership of Rinus Michels. The Dutch compensated in part for the absence of established nations like England, Hungary, Belgium and Portugal. Their exclusion ridiculed any suggestion that the world's sixteen best countries competed in West Germany.

ARGENTINA 1978

WINNERS Argentina RUNNERS-UP Holland THIRD Brazil

Other countries in finals Austria, France, Hungary, Iran, Italy, Mexico, Peru, Poland, Scotland, Spain, Sweden, Tunisia, West Germany **Total entries** 102 (16 qualifiers)
Venues Buenos Aires, Mar del Plata, Rosario, Cordoba, Mendoza
Top scorer Kempes (Argentina) 6 goals
Final (Buenos Aires): Argentina 3 (Kempes 2, Bertoni), Holland 1 (Nanninga) after extra time.
Half-time 1-0. Score after 90 minutes: 1-1 **Attendance** 77,000
Argentina Fillol, Passarella, Olguin, Galvan, Tarantini, Ardiles (Larrosa), Gallego, Oritz (Houseman), Bertoni, Luque, Kempes
Holland Jongbloed, Krol, Poortvliet, Brandts, Jansen (Suurbier), Haan, Neeskens, Van der Kerkhof W, Rep (Nanninga), Van der Kerkhof R, Resenbrink

The run of host nation victories with Argentina becoming the third host nation in four World Cups to win the trophy. For the second Final in succession, Holland were beaten, losing 3-1 after extra time against a background of ticker-tape and joyous celebration. Cruyff was no longer around to illuminate a Dutch team that fell to the goalscoring powers of Argentinian hero Mario Kempes, who scored twice in the Final. For the second time in succession England failed to reach the finals, deprived in the qualifying tournament on goal difference. So Scotland, alone again, were left to fly the British flag in Argentina, and embarrassingly they did it — once again being eliminated on goal difference.

The Scots and their ebullient but inexperienced manager, Ally MacLeod, arrived breathing hot air and left with their tails between their legs. Their morale was smashed by events in their opening 3-1 defeat by no-hopers Peru. After the game a dope test on winger Willie Johnston proved positive and Scotland sent him home in disgrace.

The Scots then slumped to a 1-1 draw with Iran, but rallied against Holland in their final match. They needed to win by a three-goal margin to progress to the second stage. That never looked likely, but, inspired by two-goal hero Archie Gemmill, Scotland managed to restore some pride with an impressive 3-2 victory.

However the final memory of 'Mundial 78' was of Argentina's doleful manager Cesar Luis Menotti lighting yet another cigarette as his captain Daniel Passarella lifted the glittering prize.

SPAIN 1982

WINNERS Italy RUNNERS-UP West Germany THIRD Poland

Other countries in finals Algeria, Argentina, Austria, Belgium, Brazil, Cameroon, Chile, Czechoslovakia, El Salvador, England, France, Honduras, Hungary, Kuwait, New Zealand, Northern Ireland, Peru, Soviet Union, Scotland, Spain, Yugoslavia **Total entries** 109 (24 qualifiers)
Venues Vigo, Coruna, Gijon, Oviedo, Barcelona, Elche, Alicante, Bilbao, Valladolid, Valencia, Zaragoza, Seville, Malaga, Madrid **Top scorer** Rossi(Italy) 6 goals
Final (Madrid) Italy 3 (Rossi, Tardelli, Altobelli), West Germany 1 (Breitner)
Half-time 0-0 **Attendance** 90,089
Italy Zoff, Bergomi, Scirea, Collovati, Cabrini, Oriali, Gentile, Tardelli, Conti, Rossi, Graziani (Altobelli [Causio])
West Germany Schumacher, Kaltz, Stielike, Forster K-H, Forster B, Dremmler (Hrubesch), Breitner, Briegel, Rummenigge (Muller), Fischer, Littbarski

The eventual winners Italy began dismally in Spain but, once past the first phase (in which they drew all three games and went through only on goal superiority over Cameroon), they developed into a formidable team. At the second stage they beat both South American giants — the holders Argentina 2-1 and the favourites Brazil 3-2. The latter was the match in which Paulo Rossi, fresh from completing a two-year ban for his part in a bribes scandal, marked his return with a sensational hat-trick. In the semi-final Rossi scored two goals that beat Poland, and in the Final he spearheaded Italy's 3-1 win against West Germany. He scored the first as Enzo Bearzot's team, captained by 40-year-old goalkeeper Dino Zoff, equalled Brazil's record of three World Cup successes.

For another record, Irish forward Norman Whiteside, at 17 years and 42 days, stole the legendary Pele's record as the youngest player ever seen in the World Cup Finals.

England made a fantastic start in Bilbao with Bryan Robson scoring after 27 seconds (a World Cup record) against France, who were beaten 3-1. But two goalless draws in the second round against West Germany and Spain, were not enough to take England into the semi-finals. Scotland, drawn in an unenviable group with Brazil and the Soviet Union were knocked out on goal difference for the third tournament in succession.

MEXICO 1986

WINNERS Argentina RUNNERS-UP West Germany THIRD France

Other countries in finals Algeria, Belgium, Brazil, Bulgaria, Canada, Denmark, England, Hungary, Iraq, Italy, Mexico, Morocco, Northern Ireland, Paraguay, Poland, Portugal, Soviet Union, Scotland, South Korea, Spain, Uruguay
Total entries 118 (24 qualifiers)
Venues Mexico City, Guadalajara, Monterrey, Puebla, Toluca, Leon, Irapuato, Queretaro, Nezahualcoytl
Top scorer Lineker (England) 6
Final (Azteca Stadium, Mexico City) Argentina 3 (Brown, Valdano, Burruchaga), West Germany 2 (Rummenigge, Voller)
Half-time 1-0 **Attendance** 114,500
Argentina Pumpido, Cuciuffo, Brown, Ruggeri, Olarticoechea, Batista, Giusti, Maradona, Burruchaga (Trobbiani), Enrique, Valdano
West Germany Schumacher, Berthold, Forster, Jakobs, Brehme, Briegel, Eder, Matthaus, Magath (Hoeness), Allofs (Voller), Rummenigge

For the second World Cup to be hosted by Mexico it was records all the way, with the 52 matches attended by 2,406,511 spectators (average 46,279) and record profits of £30,281,690. Across the world 580 million watched the Final on television, with a global audience of 12.8 billion for the whole tournament. But 132 goals produced the World Cup's lowest scoring rate at 2.54 per match, and eight players were sent off (including England's Ray Wilkins v Morocco) with a total of 133 yellow cards. Awards — Golden Ball (for tournament's outstanding player): Diego Maradona, captain of winners Argentina; Golden Boot (for top scorer): England's Gary Lineker (6 goals).

On his 41st birthday, Northern Ireland goalkeeper Pat Jennings earned his world record 119th cap v Brazil (0-3), then retired. Scotland went out when held 0-0 by ten men for 89 minutes after Uruguay's Jose Batista was dramatically sent off right at the start.

Bobby Robson's England made their exit in the quarter-final, 1-2 v Argentina, both goals for the victors by Maradona, the first clearly handball, the second a brilliant solo effort.

In a dramatic Final, Argentina led 2-0. West Germany levelled at 2-2 and, six minutes from time, Jorge Burruchaga scored the winner for the South Americans.

Overleaf: 1990 World Cup Stadium, Milan

GARDA

WORLD CUP 199

2nd ROUND

Naples Bari Turin Milan Genoa Rome Verona Bologna

WINNERS	DATE	VENUE	TIME	TEAMS	RESULT
1	June 23	Naples	4pm	B1 v A3/C3/D3	
2	June 23	Bari	8pm	A2 v C2	
3	June 24	Turin	4pm	C1 v A3/B3/F3	
4	June 24	Milan	8pm	D1 v B3/E3/F3	
5	June 25	Genoa	4pm	F2 v B2	
6	June 25	Rome	8pm	A1 v C3/D3/E3	
7	June 26	Verona	4pm	E1 v D2	
8	June 26	Bologna	8pm	F1 v E2	

QUARTER-FINALS

Florence Rome Milan Naples

	DATE	VENUE	TIME	TEAMS			RESULT
A	June 30	Florence	4pm	Winner 3	v	Winner 7	
B	June 30	Rome	8pm	Winner 5	v	Winner 6	
C	July 1	Milan	4pm	Winner 2	v	Winner 4	
D	July 1	Naples	8pm	Winner 1	v	Winner 8	